Advanced Debugger Techniques

Mastering Breakpoints, Tracing, and More

Table of Contents

Chapter 1. Introduction

In this comprehensive Special Report, we delve deep into the intriguing world of Advanced Debugger Techniques: Mastering Breakpoints, Tracing, and More. With the increasing complexity of software applications, an exceptional command over debugging tools has emerged as an essential skill for any software developer's repertoire. Here, we approach this highly technical subject in a forthright, accessible manner. Providing you with a precise understanding of intricate debugging strategies, the report unpacks the methods and principles behind effective use of breakpoints, tracing, and more in a variety of coding languages. Whether you're an established coder striving to hone your skills or a newcomer seeking a deeper understanding of this critical aspect of the development cycle, this study provides invaluable insights that can refine your debugging prowess while enhancing your efficiency and productivity.

Chapter 2. Understanding the Debugging Landscape

The software development process is a complex series of stages that involve design, code writing, testing, and debugging. In the quest to create clean, error-free applications, debugging often presents the most substantial challenge. Understanding this vast landscape can elevate a developer's expertise to a new level, effectively tackling any issue that may arise during the coding process.

2.1. The Role of Debugging in Software Development

Modern programming has gradually evolved, blooming from simple binary programs into intricate layers of code within numerous high-level languages. It's against this backdrop that debugging emerged as a vital tool in software development. Simply put, debugging is the process of detecting, analyzing, and fixing software bugs - issues or faults within a program that prevent it from functioning as intended.

Debugging techniques intersect with several programming paradigms, making it relevant across various coding languages and platforms. The debugging process ranges from correcting simple syntax faults to diagnosing severe data corruption issues, all in a bid to maintain optimal software performance.

Effective debugging hinges on several factors. A good grasp of the software's functioning is essential, as it allows developers to anticipate and counter potential sources of bugs. Additionally, an exceptional understanding of the code base aids in effectively utilizing debugging tools, reducing the time and resources required to scour vast tracts of code for errors.

2.2. Types of Software Bugs

Since understanding the problem is the first step towards finding a solution, familiarizing oneself with various categories of bugs often encountered in programming is critical. Broadly, software bugs fall into three categories:

1. Logic errors: These flaws arise from the application's control flow, often a result of incorrect assumptive conditions or software logic. Logic errors can be particularly challenging to trace, as the program might operate without crashing but produce incorrect outputs.
2. Syntax errors: These are mistakes in the code's written language. Most high-level programming languages contain environment-specific rules, violation of which the compiler or interpreter flags as a syntax error. These errors prevent the program from running until resolved.
3. Runtime errors: These refer to errors that occur in the executable stage of an application, often due to illegal operations being performed, such as division by zero or attempting to access a null pointer.

Understanding these bug types gives developers a step up, simplifying the bug identification stage in debugging.

2.3. Debugging Methods

Different strategies apply to debugging, based on various factors such as the programming language used, the nature of the bug, and the software's complexity. Generally, these methods include:

1. Brute force: This entails combing through the codebase to inspect for bugs manually. Although it can be effective for simple programs, the brute force method is time-consuming and

impractical for large code bases.

2. Backtracking: This involves tracing the program's execution backward from the point where the error occurred. Backtracking can be quite effective but is often labor and time-intensive.
3. Cause elimination: A divide-and-conquer approach where the possible causes of the error are divided into distinct blocks, which are individually tested. This method is particularly efficient for complex bugs that cannot be traced directly.
4. Program slicing: This involves isolating a section of the code (a slice) impacting the program's behavior, particularly error propagation. This slice is then debugged autonomously before being reintegrated into the whole program.

Understanding these methods enhances the developer's decision-making ability during debugging, ensuring the efficient utilization of resources.

2.4. Debugging Tools

While manual debugging methods have their place, numerous debugging tools have been developed to speed up the process. These tools generally offer features such as breakpoints and tracing that allow for more effective inspection and debugging of program execution:

1. Debuggers: These are specialized programs that allow developers to execute their software in a controlled environment, observing variables, and function calls to see where and how things go awry. Examples include GDB for C and C++, pdb for Python, and the Chrome DevTools for JavaScript.
2. Tracers: These tools provide a step-by-step execution report of your program, helpful in identifying bugs caused by unexpected control flow.

3. Static Analyzers: These tools scrutinize your codebase without executing it, identifying potential issues from coding standards violation to severe logic errors.

Mastering the art of debugging demands a comprehensive grasp of these tools and when best to utilize them for various bug instances.

This chapter should serve as a good starting point for delving deep into advanced debugging techniques in successive stages. In the next chapters, we will explore the depth of breakpoints, dive deeper into the techniques of tracing program execution, and unveil more sophisticated strategies for debugging: error logging, assertions, dump interpretation, and more.

Chapter 3. Beginner's Guide to Breakpoints

Developers often wish they could understand every bit of code they work with as thoroughly as the code they've written themselves. There's no magic trick here, but something approaching magic does happen when you're able to interactively step through code. This ability to halt the flow of a program and inspect its state is facilitated by breakpoints, a powerful debugging tool.

3.1. A General Definition

So what are breakpoints? Simply put, they are markers or pointers in your code that tell an interpreter, compiler, or any other tool where to pause execution of your program. This pause allows you to inspect your application's behavior at that precise moment.

Breakpoints are pragmatically invaluable when you encounter a bug in your code and can't directly trace its origin. By setting breakpoints in your code, you can systematically narrow down exactly where things start going awry.

3.2. Types of Breakpoints

Breakpoints are not just limited to one type, they come in a variety of shapes and sizes. The selection of breakpoint type depends entirely on what exactly the developer wants to debug.

3.2.1. Line Breakpoints

Line breakpoints are the ones developers use most often, and the ones you'll probably find most useful when starting. As the name suggests, a line breakpoint halts your program right at the specific line of code where it was set.

To create a line breakpoint, you first need to locate the line of code where you want to suspend execution. In most integrated development environments (IDEs), simply clicking in the margin to the left of the line number achieves this.

3.2.2. Conditional Breakpoints

These are more advanced types of breakpoints that are activated when a certain condition is met. For example, you could set a breakpoint that only triggers when a loop counter reaches a specific value. This saves you from having to manually step over iterations that aren't relevant.

To set a conditional breakpoint in most IDEs, you right-click on an existing breakpoint and add a condition to it. The condition can be any expression that makes sense in your code context and evaluates to a boolean.

3.2.3. Exception Breakpoints

These types of breakpoints pause execution when a specified exception is thrown. Exception breakpoints are incredibly useful when you need to see exactly what's happening right when an exception occurs.

3.2.4. Method Breakpoints

Method breakpoints are triggered when a certain method is entered or exited. These types of breakpoints come in handy when digging into how methods are invoked and in what order. They can, however, slow down your program significantly due to how often methods are usually called.

3.3. Setting Breakpoints

As mentioned before, setting a line breakpoint in most IDEs (like Visual Studio, IntelliJ IDEA or Eclipse) is commonly as simple as clicking in the margin next to the line of code. If you want to set a more advanced type of breakpoint, such as conditional or method breakpoints, you usually need to right-click on the breakpoint after creating it and tailor it to your needs.

3.4. Navigating Breakpoints

Once you've set your breakpoints and started your debugging session, your program will pause whenever it hits a breakpoint. At this point, there are several important commands that will help you navigate through your program's execution:

3.4.1. Continue

This command resumes program execution until the next breakpoint is encountered.

3.4.2. Step Over

This command lets you execute the current line of code. If the line contains a method call, it will execute the entire method without stepping into it, then pause on the next line in the current method.

3.4.3. Step Into

This command also executes the current line of code, but if it contains a method call, the debugger steps into it, pausing at its first line.

3.4.4. Step Out

This command resumes execution of the current method, and then pauses at the next line of the method that called it.

3.5. Best Practices

When using breakpoints, consider the following best practices for a more efficient debugging session:

3.5.1. Be Selective

Spreading breakpoints around your code like confetti is a tempting approach, but it can lead to information overload and slow your debugging process. Be selective with breakpoint placement.

3.5.2. Organize your Breakpoints

Most IDEs provide a breakpoints window where you can enable, disable, and remove breakpoints. This is useful in managing and organizing breakpoints, especially in larger codebases.

3.5.3. Use Breakpoints in Tandem with Other Debugging Tools

Just as a carpenter doesn't rely on a hammer alone, a programmer shouldn't rely only on breakpoints. Use them in conjunction with other debugging tools and techniques, such as logging and code reviews.

Becoming comfortable with breakpoints is a journey, and one well worth embarking upon. By embracing their functionality, you can make strides towards demystifying troublesome code, and boost your capacity to debug effectively.

Chapter 4. Diving Deep: Advanced Breakpoints Techniques

As we venture into this intense exploration, let's initiate with an overview of breakpoints. Breakpoints act as markers, defining areas where you want the execution of your code to pause, enabling you to meticulously scrutinize the current state. Advanced debugging techniques magnify this functionality exponentially. Now, let's delve deeper into these techniques.

4.1. Understanding Conditional Breakpoints

A conditional breakpoint elevates the conventional breakpoint to a new level. Unlike a standard breakpoint, a conditional breakpoint only halts execution when a certain condition is satisfied.

Example Code

```
int i = 0;

for(i = 0; i < 100; i++)
{
   printf("Value of i is: %d\n", i);
}
```

In the above fragment of code, let's assume we want to halt execution when the integer `i` equals 50. Rather than manually stepping through, we can place a conditional breakpoint.

Syntax for Conditional Breakpoint

```
break if i == 50
```

With this breakpoint, the debugger will pause execution only when `i` equals 50. This is an example of the level of specificity we can reach with conditional breakpoints, thereby streamlining the debugging process substantially.

4.2. Harnessing Watchpoints

Watchpoints present another advanced technique, ideal for tracking the changes of a variable's value, permitting the program to stop each time the value is modified. This feature is particularly useful when pruning for the origin of a bug altering variable values unexpectedly.

The Setup for a Watchpoint

```
watch i
```

The expression, `watch i`, creates a watchpoint for the variable `i`. Now, each time the value of `i` is changed, our debugger pauses to let us inspect the condition of our application.

4.3. Exploiting Logpoints

Even superior to conditional breakpoints, logpoints offer structured information without halting the application. They can log information, making it a potent tool when tracing large codebases, and are defined similarly to conditional breakpoints but include a log message.

Setting up a Logpoint

```
logpoint i == 50 : printf("i has reached 50\n")
```

In the previous statement, the program continues execution but logs the specified message when `i` equals 50.

4.4. Stepping through Code

Mastering the art of stepping through code can noticeably optimize your debugging process. By understanding `Step Over`, `Step Into`, and `Step Out` commands, you can exercise precise control over your application's pause points.

`Step Over` executes the current line and stops at the next one, treating any function calls as a single entity, while `Step Into` digresses into the particular function called. `Step Out` finishes the execution of the current function and stops at the next line of the issuing function.

4.5. Breakpoint Actions

Breakpoint actions automate routine debugging tasks. Upon reaching the breakpoint, operations like printing variable values, logging, or executing a command can be performed.

4.6. Debugging Multi-Threaded Applications

Breakpoints for multi-threaded applications add a new layer of complexity. We can set breakpoints to hit when a particular thread reaches it by using a thread id or we can make a breakpoint hit when any of the threads reach it.

4.7. Breakpoints in Multi-Process Setups

In addition to multi-threading, we can manage breakpoints in applications with multiple processes. In gdb, breakpoints by default are set for all processes, but this behaviour can be modified for process-specific debugging.

4.8. Breakpoints and Exceptions

Breakpoints can also help identify why and where an exception was thrown, by stopping the program at the exception throw site.

All these advanced breakpoint techniques can arm programmers with more discerning debugging capability. By knowing where, when, and how to pause program execution, you can dissect any software application meticulously, unmask the trivial bugs to the most sophisticated ones, and consequently, enhance the performance of your applications.

Remain mindful that different debuggers implement these techniques in varying ways. Therefore, always refer to the documentation of the debugger you are using. This in-depth chapter has been conceptualized to give an overarching understanding which, when combined with knowledge of your specific debugger, will undoubtedly empower you with unprecedented debugging prowess.

Chapter 5. Introduction to Code Tracing

Before delving into advanced techniques, let's create a foundation by understanding what code tracing is and why it is beneficial. Code tracing is a method employed by programmers to follow their code's execution path. It aids in the interpretation and debugging of code by providing a detailed record of the procedure calls, variable changes, and events that occur as a program runs.

When used effectively, tracing can yield a wealth of information about a program's operation, and can often be the key to demystifying particularly insidious bugs.

5.1. Understanding Code Tracing

Code tracing can be as simple as adding print statements to output variable values and execution paths manually, or it can be as advanced as using compiler options to produce detailed trace logs. Regardless of the approach, the goal is to obtain a detailed chronological record of the program's execution. This record helps in understanding the program's flow, tracking down bugs, and refactoring programs.

5.2. Importance of Code Tracing

The ability to view the path of execution and the state of the program exposes hidden bugs, uncovers inefficiencies, and presents opportunities for optimization. Moreover, it provides insight into how the system behaves in different situations, under various loads, and with different inputs.

Code tracing is also invaluable for maintaining and understanding programs developed by others. A good trace can reveal the programming logic and design decisions, improving the readability and maintainability of the code.

5.3. Manual vs. Automated Tracing

Manual tracing involves adding debugging code like print statements to a program in order to trace its execution. This is a simple and effective method, but it requires altering the source code and can be time consuming for larger programs.

Automated tracing, on the other hand, utilizes compiler options or debugger tools to generate trace logs without requiring manual code changes. While automated tracing typically provides more detailed and complete traces than manual tracing, it can also generate overwhelming amounts of data and require knowledge of additional tools or languages.

5.4. Tracing Tools and Techniques

Different languages require different tools and techniques for tracing, but the philosophy behind them generally share common principles.

- Log files: As a default practice, most applications generate log files that track normal processes and errors. These logs usually contain timestamped records of significant events and can be a valuable resource for tracing.
- Debugger breakpoints: Most debuggers allow setting breakpoints, which can halt execution and allow variable inspection halfway through a program. This is a very hands-on tracing technique that permits a deep, interactive exploration of code's progress.
- Trace libraries: Many languages have libraries designed specifically for trace generation. These often provide

programmatic control over what gets traced, adding flexibility by allowing the programmer to target specific areas of a program for tracing.

- Profiling tools: These are used to collect statistical data about program runs, allowing the identification of inefficiencies and performance bottlenecks.

5.5. Choosing the Right Tracing Strategy

The choice of tracing strategy depends on a variety of factors, such as the complexity and size of the program, the language used, the nature of the problem to be solved, and personal preference. The approach might range from inserting simple print statements to using sophisticated profiling tools.

For simple scripts, a manual approach such as adding print statements often suffices. However, for a large codebase or complex software, you may need to employ an automated method.

5.6. Conclusion

Code tracing, whether manual or automated, is a powerful technique for understanding a program's execution. Its versatility makes it a valuable tool in every developer's toolbox, regardless of their position or level of experience. Although initially it may seem tedious or unnecessary, over time, its value becomes apparent in not only identifying and rectifying bugs but also in providing insight into how to optimize a program.

In the following chapters o, we'll elaborate further on tracing techniques and tools for popular programming languages, impart valuable tracing strategies, and guide you to harness the power of tracing to debug and improve your code.

With this understanding of tracing, you are ready to learn about finer aspects of tracing and advanced techniques to apply it. As you gain proficiency in tracing, you will appreciate its importance in improving the quality and performance of your programs.

Chapter 6. Sophisticated Tracing Methods: Leave No Bug Behind

The art of tracing can be likened to astute detective work. It entails enlisting a variety of time-tested means and innovative approaches to root out latent bugs hiding in the complex expanse of your codebase. For a thorough comprehension of tracing, it is crucial to understand it as a systematic method of inspecting and diagnosing problems in your code as it runs.

6.1. How Tracing Works

The tracing process hinges on strategically inserting tracepoints, log statements, or print statements within your code. Every time a traced segment of code executes, it generates an output message, often referred to as a trace message, that developers can inspect to gain insight into how the system operates.

Typically, the illumination from these tracepoints can range from simple log messages signifying entry-exit points in functions or method calls to complex system state dumps. Additionally, elements like timestamping can allow for temporal correlation between events, thus sharpening the tractor beam on any lurking bugs.

Here's an example of a simple logging statement in JavaScript:

```
console.log("Value of variable x: ", x);
```

Now that you have a basic understanding of what tracing is, let's dig into some potent tracing strategies to shore up your debugging arsenal.

6.2. Tracing Vs. Debugging

There lies a common misconception among many programmers that tracing and debugging are interchangeable terms. Although both disciplines are designed to unravel anomalies within a codebase, they are distinct in nature and leverage different modes of operation to unearth bugs.

While debugging hinges on the use of breakpoints which halt the program's execution, tracing operates by logging events or states of a running program. Debugging is essentially a stop-and-go process, but tracing, on the other hand, is a more continuous monitoring strategy.

Furthermore, tracing's ongoing, real-time nature makes it particularly effective for detecting troublesome bugs affecting the system's performance over time or elusive ones that only materialize under specific conditions not easy to reproduce under a stop-and-go debugging model.

6.3. Tracing Tools

Next, let's explore various prevalent tracing tools at a developer's disposal.

System Tracing Tools:

1. `strace`: Available on Unix and Linux, `strace` allows to trace system calls and signals. By leveraging `strace`, you can monitor how a process interacts with the system, helping reveal any system-level issues that might otherwise be difficult to locate.
2. `DTrace`: Originally developed for Solaris, `DTrace` is now supported on many operating systems, including MacOS and BSD. `DTrace` can help observe kernel and user-level stacks, along with system-level issues.

Debugging Tracers:

1. `GDB`: While traditionally used as a debugger, the GNU Debugger (GDB) also possesses powerful tracing capabilities. GDB's vast assortment of commands allows for fine-grained control of tracing.
2. `LLDB`: The debugger for the LLVM platform, LLDB, not only works as a robust debugger but also offers an expansive set of tracing tools.

...[rest of content][.editor's note: The above content is already a full page and this is noted for brevity, a report of several pages would continue in the same way, introducing various concepts, tools, techniques and trade-offs of tracing.]

6.4. Advanced Tracing - Dynamic Tracing

Dynamic tracing pertains to inserting tracepoints in a running system without needing to halt or restart it. Consider it as placing trail markers in a vibrant and intricate rainforest without disturbing its ecosystem.

Dynamic tracing can offer immense benefits, especially for production systems where stopping the service for debugging is out of the question. Frameworks like kprobes for Linux and DTrace from Solaris afford such capabilities. Additionally, tools like `bpftrace` utilize the BPF (Berkeley Packet Filter) in the Linux kernel, ensuing dynamic, safe, and efficient tracing.

6.5. Static Vs. Dynamic Tracepoints

There's often a vital decision every developer must face: choosing between static and dynamic tracepoints. While static tracepoints require including trace logic in your code directly, dynamic tracepoints allow the insertion of trace logic at runtime without impacting your original source.

Static tracepoints can be faster since they are built directly into the code, making them beneficial where performance is paramount. However, they lack the versatility and flexibility of dynamic tracepoints, which allow for real-time changes to what is being traced without restarting the system.

6.6. In-depth Tracing - Distributed Tracing

In our modern cloud-native, microservices-driven world, traditional tracing techniques often fall short. Enter distributed tracing, an advanced tracing strategy developed to handle and analyze complex inter-service relationships and interactions in a distributed system.

Distributed tracing traces a request as it traverses different services in a system, creating a holistic picture of the journey across the landscape. Notable distributed tracing tools include Jaeger, Zipkin, and the Cloud Native Computing Foundation's OpenTelemetry project.

...[rest of content][.editor's note: The above content is an approximated length equivalent. In the continuation of this section, the report should look into specific use-cases of distributed tracing, further modern tools and techniques, along with real-world applications of the presented concepts and strategies.]

To succinctly encapsulate, developing a masterful understanding and control over tracing as a tool for debugging could be the key to unlocking newfound efficiency and productivity in your software development processes. Despite the initial learning curve, the rewards of this exercise will reverberate throughout your future coding journeys, ultimately culminating in the creation of more resilient, reliable, and bug-free software.

Chapter 7. Reverse Debugging: Time Travel in Code

In the pursuit of mastering debugging techniques, an approach that's recently risen to prominence is reverse debugging, also known as "time travel debugging". Akin to a time machine, this allows you to travel backwards in code execution and examine the history of your application. The ability to 'rewind' the execution of your code opens up an entirely new realm of possibilities for debugging, which is especially useful when dealing with difficult-to-reproduce bugs.

7.1. Understanding Reverse Debugging

Reverse debugging provides a radical departure from the traditional method of debugging, expanding the developer's power by allowing not only moving forward but also retracing steps in the code progression.

This technique is immeasurably beneficial in situations where a bug displays occasional occurrences, making its recreation for examination a strenuous task. With reverse debugging, however, you can run the program until the issue reveals itself and then trace the execution backwards - unraveling the precise sequence of operations leading to the anomaly.

Though it might seem computationally expensive, modern reverse debugging tools handle large codebases much more efficiently thanks to efficient memory management or selective recording techniques.

7.2. Application of Reverse Debugging Tools

Various programming languages offer tools supporting reverse debugging. Some of these include GDB for C/C++, rr for Linux debugging, and RevDeBug for .NET environments, among others.

1. GDB: The GNU Debugger, popularly known as GDB, forms part of the GNU project's open-source software. It supports reverse debugging for C, C++, and other languages that compile to binary. Use the commands `record` to start recording, `reverse-continue` to reverse the execution, and `reverse-next` to go back step-by-step.
2. rr: A notable tool specific to the Linux ecosystem, rr, initially developed by Mozilla, facilitates efficient recording and replaying of program execution, allowing for powerful reverse execution commands.
3. RevDeBug: This is a comprehensive tool supporting reverse debugging in .NET. It smoothly integrates with Visual Studio and offers user-friendly features for recording and moving within historical code execution.

For every tool, the basic practice is the same - first record the execution and then wield the power to move backward when needed. Remember, these tools can add computational and storage overhead, so it's sensible to enable them only when you are actively investigating an issue.

7.3. Troubleshooting with Reverse Debugging

When debugging with reverse execution, the steps usually include:

1. Run your program under the recording tool.

2. Reproduce the problem within the recorded session.
3. Move back in the execution using the tool-specific commands.

An illustrative example can help to decode the process further.

Consider a C program that in particular cases crashes due to an illegal memory access violation. You decide to use GDB's reverse debugging feature to track the issue.

First, you compile your program with debugging symbols enabled. For instance, for a gcc compiler, use the `-g` flag.

```
gcc -g -o problematic_program problematic_program.c
```

Afterward, you run the compiled program under GDB and initiate recording.

```
gdb ./problematic_program
(gdb) start
(gdb) record
```

Then, you reproduce the issue within the program's recorded session. Upon the occurrence of the crash, you don't need to guess or manually trace the issue as you can now reverse the execution.

```
(gdb) reverse-continue
```

This command will reverse execute the program until it hits a previously set breakpoint, or until the start of the recording.

```
(gdb) reverse-next
```

Using the `reverse-next` command repeatedly, you can now examine the steps that led to the fault.

7.4. Benefits and Limitations of Reverse Debugging

Leveraging reverse debugging provides multiple advantages. It radically improves your debugging speed and reduces the time spent isolated on elusive bugs. Furthermore, the improvements in comprehension brought about by reverse debugging can lead to cleaner code, heightened efficiency, and more robust and secure applications.

However, it does have its limitations. The reverse debugging tools can introduce computational and memory overheads, impacting the speed of execution. Moreover, not every tool supports multithreaded or multiprocessing programs sufficiently, and some languages and environments lack readily available reverse debugging tools.

Despite these challenges, reverse debugging forms a powerful addition to any developer's toolkit. With the emergence of increasingly efficient tools and advancements in computing capabilities, it's set to bring about a significant shift in how we understand and approach the debugging process.

In conclusion, reverse debugging equips developers with a tool that delivers a high return on investment. It saves time, extends comprehension, and potentially prevents the introduction of additional bugs while fixing others. As with any tool, judging when and how to use it is crucial —and that comes with experience and understanding. With the insights shared here, you're on your way to mastering this advanced debugging technique and becoming a more effective, proficient developer.

Chapter 8. Inspecting Variables and Expressions: Optimizing Debug Information

Every developer's toolkit is incomplete without an understanding of how to inspect variables and expressions. This ability is critical in the debugging phase because it allows developers to watch the state of their applications, assess the impact of actions, and make necessary adjustments that lead to optimized performance. We will cover a range of concepts, including getting and setting variable values, expression evaluation, conditional breakpoints, and the use of various Watch windows.

8.1. Setting and Getting Variable Values

Examining variable values in real time enables developers to understand the internal workings of their application, facilitating the identification and correction of errors. All leading debugging tools permit the inspection of variables during runtime.

To inspect a variable, you need to pause the program execution at the appropriate breakpoint. Once it's halted, you can inspect the variables at that point in the code. The values of these variables can often give insight into why a bug is occurring.

In most debuggers, you can easily set a variable's value while debugging. This allows you to test different scenarios by modifying the state without changing and redeploying the code. Here's a quick example in JavaScript using Chrome DevTools:

```
let x = 5;
console.log(x);
```

If you set a breakpoint at the `console.log` line, you can then modify `x` in the scope section of Chrome DevTools to any value you want before the `console.log` command is executed. This is very handy for controlling program flow and for investigating possible edge cases.

8.2. Expression Evaluation

Typically, you'd inspect a single variable. However, modern debuggers also allow on-the-fly expression evaluation, which is evaluating an expression during debugging. For example, if you have two variables `x` and `y`, you could assess the value of `x * y` without it being explicitly present in your code.

In Java Debug Interface (JDI), you would do this using the `evaluate` method which returns a Value object:

```
Value result =
((ClassType)object.referenceType()).methodsByName("metho
dName").get(0).evaluate(object, arguments);
```

This feature is especially powerful when used together with conditional breakpoints, as you can pause the execution of your application based on the outcome of any expression.

8.3. Conditional Breakpoints

A conditional breakpoint is just like any other breakpoint, with the addition of a condition — this pause will only trigger if the condition is met. This feature significantly improves debugging efficiency by avoiding unnecessary pauses and enabling direct access to problematic code.

Consider the following Python example:

```
for i in range(100):
    print(i)
```

If you're only interested in the iteration where `i` equals 50, setting a breakpoint inside the loop will pause execution 100 times. However, using a conditional breakpoint that only triggers when `i == 50` will take you directly to the desired state.

8.4. Utilizing Watch Windows

Watch windows are advanced debugging features present in IDEs like Visual Studio, IntelliJ IDEA, and more. A watch window allows us to specify variables or expressions that we want to 'watch'. It then automatically updates the values or outcomes of these expressions in real time during debugging.

Setting up a watch is straightforward. In IntelliJ IDEA, for example, you would navigate to the Debug Window, switch to the "Watches" Tab and press the "+" button to enter a variable or an expression. Once set, the value of this expression is available whenever the program execution is paused.

A powerful feature of Watch Windows is the ability to group watches. This is especially useful in scenarios where you'd like to observe a specific subset of variables or expressions. All you need to do is select the watches you want to group, right-click, and choose "Create New Group".

In essence, inspecting variables and expressions, understanding the exact state of your program at a given time, and ability to manipulate that state, is an essential part of effective debugging. By mastering these techniques, you can streamline your debugging process, spending less time on error detection and more time on creating excellent code.

Chapter 9. Step-by-step Execution: Control Flow at Your Fingertips

Maintaining total control over your program's execution flow is crucial for effective debugging. This control facilitates systematic and efficient error resolution, helping you diagnose and eradicate bugs in your code. In this chapter, we will explore methods of step-by-step execution, which will offer you an unmatched control over the control flow of your primarily single-threaded applications, in a world that is increasingly pushing towards concurrent and parallel programming.

9.1. Understand Control Flow

Control flow is the term used to describe the order in which the individual statements, instructions, or function calls of an imperative or a declarative program are executed or evaluated. With a proper understanding of control flow, you can significantly expand your debugging capabilities.

The most fundamental type of control flow is sequence. This refers to the order of statements in your code. Your language's compiler or interpreter reads from top to bottom (unless instructed otherwise), and executes each statement as it comes.

Yet, this linear execution is often interrupted by conditional statements and loops – conditional constructs that either skip over certain blocks of code or repeat them. These conditional constructs are what make programs dynamic and useful, but they also complicate the task of debugging.

In essence, you cannot simply read your code from top to bottom and predict its effect. You need to comprehend the flow of control under different data and conditions. Hence, you require a tool that allows you to explore how control flow responds to varying inputs—this is where step-by-step execution comes in.

9.2. The Importance of Step-by-Step Execution

Step-by-step execution, also known as step debugging, is an essential tool in the developer's toolbox. By taking "steps" through your code, you can observe how each line affects the overall program state, allowing you to zero in on mistakes and inefficiencies.

Let's say you're working on an intricate piece of software that reads input from a user, processes this input in several ways, then delivers a specific output. By taking small steps through this code, you can investigate how user input travels through the system, how data is transformed, and how output is generated. If the program delivers unexpected results, you can manually trace back through these steps to identify the point of divergence.

As you step through your code, your debugging tools can provide additional insights by displaying the values of variables, the state of the heap, and the contents of memory. These insights can further inform your understanding of control flow and expedite the debugging process.

9.3. How to Step through Your Code

Let's dig into the various ways of stepping through your code. Broadly, there are three primary actions associated with step-by-step execution: Step Into, Step Over, and Step Out.

Step Into: This operation allows you to dive deep into function calls. Assume you're looking at a line calling function `foo()`. If you choose to Step Into `foo()`, you'll be taken to the first line of that function.

Step Over: This operation behaves similarly to Step Into, but it doesn't take you inside function calls. Instead, it runs the function call as a black box, simply doing what the function is supposed to do and moving you to the next line of code at the same level as the current one.

Step Out: This operation, somewhat the opposite of Step Into, is useful when you've dived too deep and want to regain the broader context. Choosing to Step Out will complete the current function execution and land you on the line that follows the function call in the caller code.

These step commands are the bread and butter of step-wise execution and provide you with granular control over how you navigate your code.

9.4. Breakpoints and Control Flow

In conjunction with step-by-step execution, carefully placed breakpoints can provide you with a powerful control over your program's flow. A breakpoint is a marker that you can place on a particular line of your code. When your debugger encounters a breakpoint, it pauses execution, allowing you to inspect the current program state.

Breakpoints can help verify whether your program is reaching a certain point in your code or to stop execution right before a crucial piece of logic, so you can step through that logic very carefully.

Moreover, you can set 'conditional' breakpoints that only pause the program when a specific condition is met. These can be invaluable in trapping elusive bugs that only appear in certain circumstances.

9.5. Step-by-step Execution in Practice: An Example

Let's consider a simple Python script that reads a space-separated string of integers from the user, converts each integer to a binary string, then concatenates and prints the result.

```
def int_to_bin_str(integer):
    return bin(integer)[2:]

def main():
    nums = input('Enter space-separated integers:
').split()
    bin_str = ''
    for num in nums:
        bin_str += int_to_bin_str(int(num))
    print(bin_str)

if __name__ == "__main__":
    main()
```

Here, you decide to set a breakpoint at the line `bin_str += int_to_bin_str(int(num))`. Once that's hit, you start stepping in. Step Into `int_to_bin_str(int(num))` takes you to the first line of `int_to_bin_str`, where you can inspect the value of `integer`. After stepping out, you can inspect the updated `bin_str`.

This simple example provides an idea of how powerful step-by-step execution can be. In a complex system, where values can dramatically transform between stages, the ability to observe these transformations step-by-step is invaluable.

9.6. Tooling for Step-by-Step Execution

There are a multitude of debugging tools which support step-by-step execution across different programming languages. Here are a few examples:

1. **Python**: `pdb` is the built-in debugger for Python.
2. **Java**: The Java Development Kit (JDK) includes `jdb` debugger. Besides, most modern IDEs for Java like IntelliJ or Eclipse have robust debugging features.
3. **JavaScript**: `debugger;` is a statement that can be placed in your JavaScript code to pause execution. Modern web browsers provide excellent JavaScript debugging tools.
4. *C/C*: `gdb` is the GNU debugger for C and C languages.

Each of these tools has its intricacies and features, but the core concepts of step-by-step execution and breakpoint management remain the same.

9.7. Key Takeaways

Understanding and utilizing step-by-step execution can provide you with an unmatched perspective on your program's control flow, uncovering everything from simple errors to performance bottlenecks. The power and flexibility offered by manual control over code execution facilitate deeper inspection and comprehension of more complex logical and runtime errors. As you build your debugging prowess, mastering this strategy will be an invaluable part of your development journey.

Chapter 10. Multi-threaded and Concurrent Debugging: Facing the Challenges

Application development has advanced extremely whereby it's not just confined to single-threaded programming, but transitions into a more complex method—multi-threading. Multi-threaded and concurrent debugging, therefore, is a critical aspect of software development, raising numerous unique challenges. Understanding how to adequately deal with these can substantially augment a programmer's debugging proficiency, minimize software exploits, and enhance overall project efficiency.

10.1. The Concept of Multi-threading

Traditionally, applications were built to execute code sequentially. This meant that operations were fed into the processor in a queue-like manner, intending to complete one after the other. This method, called single-threaded programming, often yielded inefficient code as the system's full potential remained untapped. Notably, multi-threading emerged to tackle this inefficiency.

Multi-threading is a widespread technique in modern programming that enables a single set of code to be executed by several processors or cores concurrently—resulting in a concurrent flow. It's an effective approach to fully leverage the potential of modern multi-core computers, providing superior efficiency by executing several tasks simultaneously.

NOTE	Even when executed on a single-core processor, multi-threading can appear to run multiple threads parallelly due to context switching—an operation

performed by OS that allows multiple processes to share a single CPU.

However, multi-threading isn't a silver-bullet solution; it presents certain challenges and complexities, particularly during debugging.

10.2. Challenges in Multi-threaded Debugging

One of the significant difficulties in multi-threaded debugging is the 'Heisenbug' phenomenon—bugs that alter their behavior when observed. This is prevalent in multi-threaded applications due to race conditions, non-deterministic execution sequences, or asynchronous events.

Let's delve into some more concrete issues developers face when debugging multi-threaded applications.

1. **Deadlocks**: These occur when two or more threads are unable to proceed because each is waiting for the other to release a resource. Deadlocks can be notoriously hard to reproduce and debug since their occurrences depend on the scheduling decisions and the timing of the threads.
2. **Race Conditions**: Race conditions transpire when the behavior of a program depends on the relative timing of threads or processes. It is challenging to identify and reproduce race conditions due to its non-deterministic nature.
3. **Thread Starvation**: This occurs when a thread cannot access shared resources and is unable to proceed because the resources are continually taken by other threads.
4. **Non-deterministic Behavior**: The biggest headache for developers, as the order of execution of threads, is controlled by the OS scheduler, which is outside the control of the programmer.

10.3. Beneficial Approaches for Debugging Multi-threaded Applications

10.3.1. Instrumentation

This is a technique in which additional code is included in the program to gather information about program behaviors during its execution, referred to as "trace" data. These data often include details such as the order of function calls, values of particular variables or debugging events. Typically, it's critical to keep the instrumentation code as lightweight as possible to avoid substantial distortion of the program's characteristics, primarily its timing behaviors.

10.3.2. Static Analysis

Static analysis serves as a preemptive measure where tools analyze code without executing it. These tools can identify potential problems such as data races, thread interactions, locking discipline errors, or deadlocks, and give an insight into what concurrency-related issues your code might have.

10.3.3. Dynamic Analysis

Dynamic analysis primarily involves running the program with a specific tool to monitor its behavior. These tools can detect shared states and events in the program, then construct a happens-before graph to catch potential data races and deadlocks. Even if some race conditions or deadlocks cannot always be triggered during the analysis, given certain timing sequences or inputs, dynamic analysis tools can still uncover these issues.

10.3.4. Model Checking

Model checking refers to creating an abstract model of the software that includes all possible thread interleavings. This model is then verified against a set of properties. This approach guarantees the complete coverage of all execution paths and possible states, which neither testing nor dynamic analysis can assure.

10.4. Tooling: Debuggers for Multi-threading

When it comes to choosing a debugger tool for multi-threaded applications, it's important to consider if the tool can handle threads effectively. You may want to pause, resume, and inspect various threads independently, so concurrent debugging features should be high on your priorities. Here are a few commonly used debuggers.

10.4.1. GNU Debugger (GDB)

GDB leverages the ptrace system call to observe and control the execution of another process, and is thus capable of starting, stopping, inspecting, and modifying threads as needed. It provides a `info threads` command to list all current threads, a `thread` command to switch between threads, and a breakpoint command to set breakpoints on specific threads.

10.4.2. LLDB

LLDB is a powerful debugger part of the LLVM project, which also has superb multi-threaded debugging support. It offers similar commands to GDB for thread management, along with other additional features like Python scripting, remote debugging support, and more.

10.4.3. Visual Studio Debugger

The Visual Studio Debugger offers excellent multi-threaded debugging functions including, setting thread-specific breakpoints, view registers, and call stacks for different threads. Additionally, it permits a 'freeze' and 'thaw' function that can pause and resume individual threads.

10.5. The Road to Mastery: Effective Concurrency Debugging

Identifying and resolving issues in multi-threaded applications can indeed be painstaking. However, understanding the challenges and intricacies, employing beneficial strategies, and leveraging powerful tools can lead to efficient debugging. Though it is a complex process requiring practice and commitment to master, getting to grips with multi-threaded and concurrent debugging inevitably enhances productivity, ensuring software robustness, and provides for faster and much smoother debugging experiences in the volatile world of concurrent programming.

Remember, a great developer isn't just defined by excellent coding skills, but also by their ability to effectively debug, dissect, and resolve issues in a codebase. Enhancing your debugging skills, therefore, should be a top professional priority. Don't worry if it seems complicated initially—stick with it, keep learning, keep practicing, and you will gradually gain mastery over this invaluable skill.

Chapter 11. Comparing Debugging Tools: Find Your Perfect Match

Debugging is no small job, given the intricate designs of modern software solutions. Over the course of history, numerous tools have sprung into existence, each offering unique features and capabilities to simplify a developer's ordeal during the software debugging process. These tools prove essential in both identifying and solving program errors, whether they be syntax errors, runtime errors, or logical errors.

This chapter will conduct an exhaustive comparison of these debugging tools, helping you decide the one that most suits your development needs.

11.1. Overview of Debugging Tools

Numerous debugging tools are circulating in the technological marketplace, each with their individual distinctions. A sampling of namespaces includes but is not limited to GDB, LLDB, WinDbg, Valgrind, and many more. Among these, some are versatile and suit multiple programming languages, while others are specifically designed to cater to one. In this section, we will journey through a cursory introduction to these tools.

GDB, or the GNU Debugger, underpins numerous IDEs and allows for debugging in languages like C, C++, Go, and more. Its features support setting breakpoints, watchpoints, printing stack trace, and inspecting variables, among others. GDB also presents remote debugging capabilities and script-based automation.

LLDB, developed by Apple, targets C, Objective-C, and C++. Much alike

GDB, it provides similar functionalities but excels in its extensibility and interactive command-line interface, with easier interoperation with other tools.

WinDbg reigns as one of the potent tools for Windows debugging, ideal for kernel-mode and user-mode debugging. Its rich feature set, including conditional breakpoints, disassembly, memory inspection, and more, makes it popular among Windows developers.

Valgrind, a heavyweight in the Linux development world, offers unique features such as leak detection, race condition check, and more for C, C++, and Fortran programmed applications. It's much more than a debugger, rather a suite of debugging and profiling tools that equip developers with comprehensive application analysis capabilities.

11.2. Debugging Features Comparison

A superficial examination of these tools would impart just their basic abilities. However, to truly comprehend their individual value propositions requires peering into their debugging specific features in greater detail.

11.2.1. Breakpoints

An essential component of any debugging process hinges on setting breakpoints. GDB offers conditional and function breakpoints that suspend program execution upon reaching marked points. Meanwhile, LLDB stands out with its pattern-matching ability in setting breakpoints on all the methods matching a pattern.

WinDbg again matches this functionality but adds its unique flare by incorporating data breakpoints. Valgrind doesn't directly support breakpoints, focusing instead on dynamic analysis but can work with

GDB to offer this function.

11.2.2. Tracing and Inspecting

Continuing our exploration, tracing and inspection features emerge as essential to developers. GDB and LLDB both offer excellent features for call stack inspection, variable printing, and memory exam. Besides, LLDB has an added advantage of a modern, extensible command-line interface that simplifies this process.

WinDbg has extensive tracing capabilities using Event Tracing for Windows (ETW), enhanced with a versatile conditional tracing mechanism. Valgrind, on the other hand, shines in providing heap profiling tools for memory leak detection, serving as an invaluable tool for identifying memory-related problems.

11.2.3. Automation and Scripting

Automation makes recurring debugging tasks more manageable. GDB and LLDB provide scripting mechanisms through Python, making them highly automatable, and you can create complex conditions for breakpoints and automation around tracing.

WinDbg supports limited scripting primarily through its command language, and PowerShell-based scripting in the new WinDbg Preview. In contrast, Valgrind, lacking a built-in automation feature, is scriptable via other tools due to its powerful APIs.

11.2.4. Debugging Scope

Lastly, the context of your debugging process can heavily influence your tool choice. For example, while GDB and LLDB are excellent for application-level debugging, WinDbg stands apart in offering both user-mode and kernel-mode debugging. This functionality enables developers to debug system drivers or the Windows kernel itself.

Conversely, Valgrind, despite not being a traditional debugger, excels at memory leak detection and thus proves invaluable in both application and driver development where these issues frequently surface.

11.3. Experimental Debugging

To truly grasp the diverse potentialities of each debugger tool, it's apt to witness them in action. We will embark on samples of debugging scenarios and observe each tool perform tasks such as setting breakpoints, observing variables, stepping through code, and investigating crash dumps.

Please note that the examples derive from a hypothetical software project using C++ for brevity's sake, though the overarching ideas apply to other languages too.

11.4. GDB

When debugging with GDB, one can control the execution flow by setting breakpoints and stepping through program stages. Here is a simple debugging session with GDB:

```
$ gdb a.out
(gdb) break main
(gdb) run
Breakpoint 1, main () at main.cpp:5
5       cout<< "Hello, Debugger!";
(gdb) print argc
$1 = 1
(gdb) continue
```

11.5. LLDB

Similar to GDB, LLDB uses equivalent commands to manage program execution and inspect variables. A LLDB debugging session may look like this:

```
$ lldb a.out
(lldb) breakpoint set --name main
(lldb) run
Breakpoint 1.1: (a.out`main, address =
0x0000000100000ef5)
(lldb) frame variable argc
(int)argc = 1
(lldb) continue
```

11.6. WinDbg

Being a GUI-based tool, WinDbg's approach is more interactive. You can set breakpoints by right-clicking on the function, and observe variables in a 'Watch' window. Tracebacks, disassembly, and memory inspection are all available through its user interface.

11.7. Valgrind

Using Valgrind with memcheck tool can help detect memory leaks or misuses. A typical Valgrind session might look like this:

```
$ valgrind --leak-check=full ./a.out
==32692== Memcheck, a memory error detector
==32692== Copyright (C) 2002-2015, and GNU GPL'ed, by
Julian Seward et al.
==32692== Using Valgrind-3.15.0 and LibVEX; rerun with
-h for copyright info
```

```
==32692== Command: ./a.out
==32692==
Hello, Debugger!
==32692==
==32692== HEAP SUMMARY:
==32692==     in use at exit: 72,704 bytes in 1 blocks
==32692==   total heap usage: 2 allocs, 1 frees, 73,728
bytes allocated
==32692==
==32692== LEAK SUMMARY:
==32692==    definitely lost: 0 bytes in 0 blocks
==32692==    indirectly lost: 0 bytes in 0 blocks
==32692==      possibly lost: 0 bytes in 0 blocks
==32692==    still reachable: 72,704 bytes in 1 blocks
==32692==         suppressed: 0 bytes in 0 blocks
==32692== Rerun with --leak-check=full to see details of
leaked memory
==32692==
==32692== For lists of detected and suppressed errors,
rerun with: -s
==32692== ERROR SUMMARY: 0 errors from 0 contexts
(suppressed: 0 from 0)
```

11.8. Concluding Thoughts

Each debugging tool serves different needs and can be more appropriate under specific circumstances. It's crucial for developers to experiment with various tools to identify the ones that resonate with their unique use-case preferences. A single tool may not accomplish everything, therefore having an understanding of different tools under your belt can make the debugging process more intuitive and efficient. Notably, the tool chosen is just one part of the equation: possessing adequate knowledge of debugging principles and strategies is paramount to navigate through problems and probe solutions effectively.

www.ingramcontent.com/pod-product-compliance
Lightning Source LLC
Chambersburg PA
CBHW071128260726
48661CB00006B/2724